THE
LANDSCAPES
OF
CHESHIRE

ALAN NOVELLI

COUNTRYSIDE BOOKS
NEWBURY, BERKSHIRE

First published 2004
© Alan Novelli, 2004

COUNTRYSIDE BOOKS
3 Catherine Road
Newbury, Berkshire

To view our complete range of books,
please visit us at
www.countrysidebooks.co.uk

ISBN 1 85306 874 8

*To my daughters, Lauren and Sophie,
who have inspired the words
and pictures that follow.*

Picture on page 1 shows the Mow Cop in autumn,
the picture on page 5 is of the Cheshire Cat pub sign at Christleton,
and page 80 shows the Cheshire Plain
Map on page 4 by Trevor Yorke

Designed by Peter Davies, Nautilus Design

Produced through MRM Associates Ltd., Reading
Typeset by Techniset Typesetters, Newton-le-Willows
Printed in Italy

Contents

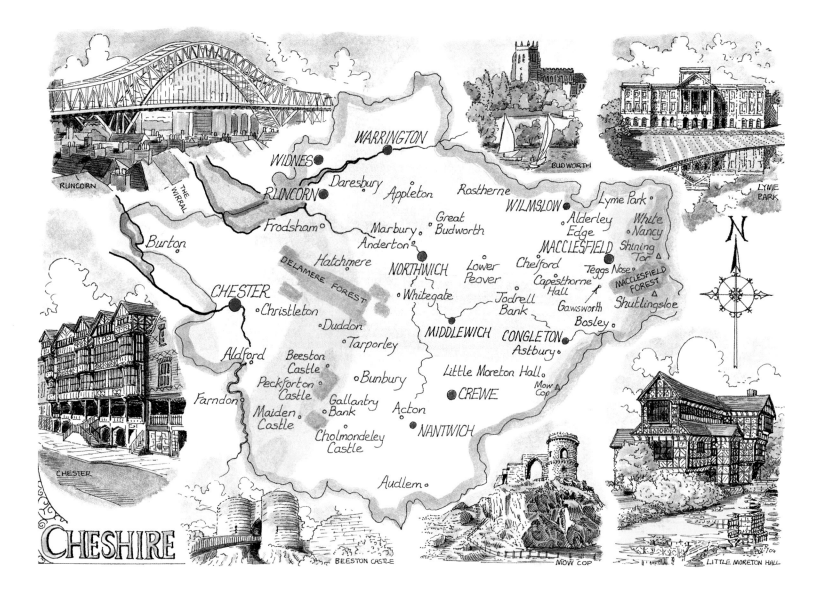

RUNCORN

WARRINGTON

WIDNES

BUDWORTH

LYME PARK

THE WIRRAL

Daresbury

Appleton

Rostherne

RUNCORN

WILMSLOW

Lyme Park

Frodsham

Marbury

Great
Budworth

Alderley
Edge

White
Nancy

Burton

Anderton

MACCLESFIELD

Shining
Tor

DELAMERE FOREST

Hatchmere

NORTHWICH

Lower
Peover

Chelford

Teggs
Nose

MACCLESFIELD
FOREST

CHESTER

Whitegate

Capesthorne
Hall

Shutlingsloe

Christleton

Jodrell
Bank

Gawsworth

Duddon

Bosley

CHESTER

Tarporley

MIDDLEWICH

CONGLETON

Aldford

Beeston
Castle

Astbury

Little Moreton Hall

Farndon

Peckforton
Castle

Bunbury

Mow
Cop

CREWE

Maiden
Castle

Gallantry
Bank

Acton

Cholmondeley
Castle

NANTWICH

Audlem

CHESHIRE

BEESTON CASTLE

MOW COP

LITTLE MORETON HALL

N

FOREWORD

Beauty is Nature's brag, and must be shown
In courts, at feasts, and at high solemnities
Where most may wonder at the workmanship …

Comus, JOHN MILTON, 1608–74

Cheshire – a county of contrasts. To the east, rugged rolling Peak District scenery is encased by lines of dry stone walling that meander their way nonchalantly to summits with grand names such as Shining Tor and Shutlingsloe. From here we travel westward, descending onto the wide expanse of the famed Cheshire Plain that envelopes the rest of the county, punctuated only by irregular sections of a central sandstone ridgeline stretching from Peckforton in the south to the hills of Helsby and Frodsham in the north.

Bustling, thronging market towns, home to spiralling populations, rapidly give way to the peace and tranquillity of Cheshire's chocolate-box villages with unending appeal and enchantment. Magnificent castles, grand halls and fairytale cottages are found nestling side by side with historic black and white 'magpie' half-timbered houses that seemingly pepper the landscape at every turn.

To adequately convey this county's remarkable scenery, with changes seen throughout its four seasons, has taken many painstaking hours of patience and devotion. Capturing misty fields and fog-filled valleys in the pale light of early morning, through to the final but often elusive golden rays of sunlight striking the landscape before the

sun's orb sinks relentlessly once more beneath the distant horizon, has been a labour of love.

The towns and cities of Cheshire have been portrayed in countless books, but here you will find inspirational images devoted to village life and the landscapes surrounding them. From the dizzy heights of Beeston and Peckforton castles, rising 500 ft above the Cheshire Plain to the expanses of water contained within the county's meres and reservoirs, all will be revealed at their most appealing.

Who is this book for?

The answer is simply for anyone with a love of our fair county.

With the current rapid expansion of our towns and cities, forever encroaching and swallowing more of Cheshire's green belt land, this book is intended to serve as a visual celebration of how magnificent our county is today, before more is lost tomorrow. As hectic lifestyles become the norm for most of us, these pictures attempt to display the county's true beauty and character, so easily overlooked as we busy ourselves with life's daily chores. If it allows a greater appreciation of Cheshire's landscape – it has served its purpose well.

Alan Novelli

CHESHIRE'S PEAK DISTRICT

I come from haunts of coot and hern,
I make a sudden sally
And sparkle out among the fern,
To bicker down a valley.

The Brook, ALFRED, LORD TENNYSON, 1809–92

What is in a name? Well, when it comes to Cheshire's own slice of the Peak District National Park, the names provide plentiful clues to features associated with this region. Windgather Rocks, Whitehills and Whetstone Ridge are a few that provide an inkling of the inhospitable weather conditions prevalent in this striking area of the county – with little to obstruct the flow of nature's harsh winds, they bite deep into the trees, fields and outcrops of rock contained here.

Although the low-lying Cheshire Plain often escapes the cruel grip of winter's snow, the same can clearly not be said for the rolling hills and peaks forming the eastern boundary of Cheshire. The winter months regularly see these slopes blanketed with a pristine covering of snow, and, when viewed from the lower elevations of the county, they provide an intensely pleasing backdrop.

Another unusual, but this time misleading name, is that of Wildboarclough village. Many people would have you believe that it was so called because it was the location of Britain's last boar hunt, but this is merely folklore. In fact the name is derived from the usually placid Clough Brook, which meanders its way gently down the valley through the centre of the village. After a heavy rainstorm, this tranquil stream rapidly becomes a raging torrent likened to the temperament of a wild boar! In 1989 one particularly fierce deluge wrought devastation on the tiny hamlet, uprooting trees and sweeping cattle miles down the valley.

One of the grandest names in this region has to be that of Shining Tor (*inset*). The highest point in Cheshire, at over 1,800 ft, its craggy summit stands like a sentinel, dominating the skyline above Lamaload Reservoir to the east of Macclesfield. Popular with

ramblers, the main path from its summit falls away toward the unusually named Cat and Fiddle Inn, which at 1,659 ft is certainly the highest and probably the most famous public house in the county. Situated on the main Macclesfield to Buxton road and boasting magnificent views of the surrounding moorland, it has been quenching the thirst of its patrons since the early 1800s.

No matter what the name, one can be absolutely certain that this popular area provides some of the most stunning vistas to be enjoyed anywhere in the county.

MACCLESFIELD FOREST

*I like trees because they seem more resigned to
the way they have to live than other things do.*

WILLA CATHA, 1873–1947, American novelist

Three miles south-east of Macclesfield is the area known as Macclesfield Forest (*opposite*). Today, the name is most commonly associated with the densely covered coniferous plantations carpeting the hillsides above Ridgegate and Trentabank reservoirs that lie at the current heart of the forest. This was not always the case, however.

Macclesfield Forest, like the forest of Mondrum and Mara (Delamere) mentioned later in this book, was a former royal hunting ground established by the Norman Earls of Chester. Covering vast swathes of the landscape, it was granted a royal charter in 1237 and became subject to the harsh forest laws. Today, the forest is a thick mass of green foliage but, in the Middle Ages, it would have appeared very different, with semi scrubland interspersed with traditional British trees. It continued like this until the latter part of the 14th century when a meteoric rise in the demand for timber took place and the inevitable deforestation that accompanied it.

Nowadays, Macclesfield Forest grosses an area in excess of 1,000 acres, incorporating hill farms, coniferous forest, windswept ridges and moorland. It is also the name given to the tiny isolated hamlet of a few houses and farms located around Forest Chapel (*inset*) on its south-eastern border.

Standing at a height of 1,300 ft above sea level the current chapel, also known as the Church of Saint Stephen, has stood firm against the harshest of Cheshire weather since 1834 when it replaced an earlier building dating from 1673. Forest Chapel's main claim to fame lies in its annual 'Rushbearing Ceremony', a custom which sees plaited reeds and flowers adorning the chapel's doorways and interior, whilst freshly cut rushes are strewn upon the floor. The tradition originates from a time when the chapel had no pews and the rushes would provide warmth in winter for those kneeling upon its stone floor. These days this annual event is performed on the first Sunday following 12th August, and if the weather is fair huge crowds throng to attend the service.

SHUTLINGSLOE

One sees great things from the valley; only small things from the peak.

The Hammer of God, G.K. CHESTERTON, 1874–1936

Spell binding scenery abounds within Cheshire's own slice of the Peak District National Park, but entirely worthy of its own mention is the mighty Shutlingsloe. Towering above the village of Wildboarclough and visible from many miles distant, it is one of the few really true 'peaks' in the park. Known locally as Cheshire's 'Matterhorn' – for such is its shape – it rises gracefully to a height of 1,659 ft above sea level.

On a clear day the strenuous climb to Shutlingsloe's majestic summit is well rewarded with spectacular views, to the west, across the entire Cheshire Plain and, to the east, across the rolling landscape of the National Park.

The most popular route to the top begins at Trentabank Reservoir in the heart of Macclesfield Forest. Heading south, the track winds steeply uphill until the walker emerges from the shadowy treeline, some 300 ft below Shutlingsloe's apex. Here one discovers superb views of the peak, particularly on a crisp early winter's evening when golden rays of sunlight illuminate its snow-laden pinnacle (*inset*).

Only hardy animals survive and prosper in this harshest of Cheshire regions. Weather-embattled sheep can be seen grazing all year round on the steep slopes of Shutlingsloe, penned into their fields by lines of locally quarried gritstone walling that seemingly cascade from its summit. This same gritstone has served generations of locals who have constructed the many barns and traditional farmhouses set into this bleak but beautiful landscape.

For the best views of Shutlingsloe, one need do no more than drive along the main A54 road from Congleton to Buxton. Here its magnificent spectacle, often framed by distorted trees with their knarled, twisted and windswept branches, provides one with a full appreciation of why this particular peak is held so fondly in the minds of Cheshire people.

TEGG'S NOSE

Human subtlety ... will never devise an invention more beautiful, more simple or more direct than does Nature, because in her inventions nothing is lacking, and nothing is superfluous.

Notebooks, LEONARDO DA VINCI, 1452–1519

Tegg's Nose is home to the mythical giant Tegg, who was able to crush huge boulders with his bare hands. In an area long associated with quarrying, it is easy to imagine how such a legend might be born.

Today, though, quarrying is a thing of the past on this windswept peak on the edge of Cheshire's Peak District. Where opencast scars on the landscape were once prevalent, we now find most covered with dense heathers that burst into a resplendent display of purple during the height of summer.

The view from the summit of Tegg's Nose (*opposite*) is astounding, with panoramic vistas in almost every direction. Looking east we find the towering form of Shutlingsloe rising above the pine-clad slopes of Macclesfield Forest, which then tumbles towards the still blue waters of Ridgegate Reservoir nestling in the valley below. A further short stroll around the wide 1,200 ft high peak brings us to a new and even more striking vantage point encompassing breathtaking southerly views over many of the county's most famous hills. Bosley Minn, The Cloud, Mow Cop and Croker Hill with its landmark telecommunications mast, all tower above a typical Cheshire picture-postcard scene made up of pretty villages, characteristic sheep farms and mile upon mile of dry stone walling.

From this same position, one need only turn clockwise through 90 degrees to take in another pleasing yet altogether different vision of the county, where a magnificent uninterrupted view of Cheshire's plain is offered, broken only by the distant landmark of Jodrell Bank's white radio telescope.

Whilst the tantalising views offered from the summit of Tegg's Nose are very special, they do not really display the majesty of the hill itself and for this one should travel to the outskirts of the village of Langley. Here, in the shadow of the peak, one discovers a delightful scene where the scree-clad, tree-lined slopes of this interesting hill are reflected in the calming waters of Bottoms Reservoir (*inset*). October is a particularly pleasing month to take in the splendour of this image, when the vibrant hues and colours of autumn present an inspirational display of nature at her very finest.

Lyme Hall and Lyme Park, Disley

Architecture, of all the arts,
Is the one which acts the most slowly,
But the most surely, on the soul.

Ernest Dimnet, 1866–1954, French priest, writer and lecturer

Ancestral home of the Legh family for over 600 years and now managed by the National Trust, Lyme Park (*opposite*) is a favourite day out for Cheshire folk. Located close to the village of Disley, the Lyme Estate encompasses over 1,400 acres of scenic splendour, including heather-rich open moors, dense woodland and impeccable formal gardens. Numerous nature trails wind their way through the many wooded areas with delightful names, including Lantern Wood and Knightslow Wood.

These trails, with their high aspect, surprise the explorer by sporadically presenting clearings containing follies or with panoramic views out over the Cheshire countryside.

Seen from many places within the park, and the jewel in Lyme's crown, is the Gothic-looking, 16th-century Lyme Hall. Familiar to many as 'Pemberley' in a BBC adaptation of Jane Austen's novel *Pride and Prejudice*, this is perhaps the greatest of Cheshire's grand halls. It is open to the public, and its southerly aspect contains a portico of four giant pillars designed by the Italian architect Giacomo Leoni, looking out over manicured lawns and gardens set around a 'reflection lake'.

Perhaps the best time to visit these gardens is in late spring, when the famous bulbs in the Dutch Garden explode into a tantalising blaze of colour.

Standing to the north of this Palladian mansion and set upon a windswept hill is a former hunting lodge known as The Cage (*inset*).

Probably dating from the early Elizabethan era, this was used as a vantage point to follow the hunting of the red and fallow deer that make the estate their home. From its perfectly square base, the walls of The Cage reach perpendicularly skywards, presenting a stark contrast to the barren hillside it crowns.

KERRIDGE HILL AND WHITE NANCY

England – a happy land we know,
Where follies naturally grow.

The Ghost, CHARLES CHURCHILL, 1731–64

A small farming community set high upon a hillside, Kerridge is an outpost of the former industrial cotton-weaving town of Bollington, and, on a clear day, Kerridge Hill offers a panoramic outlook over the whole county (*inset*).

Punctuated by the famous public footpath known as the Gritstone Trail, this elongated hilltop is popular with walkers in the region for the magnificent views presented over its entire length. Summer sees

bright yellow gorse bushes peppering its entirety and vying for position amongst the fields and dry stonewalls that herald the change of landscape towards the higher Pennine range of hills.

Situated on the very northern edge of this escarpment, seemingly clinging on to its precarious position, is the well-known folly of White Nancy (*opposite*). Visible from many miles around, this folly has been a feature of the hillside for nearly 200 years, its position and purpose having long been the subject of much argument and discussion amongst the local population. It was actually built as a summerhouse in 1817 by John Gaskell of Ingersley Hall to commemorate the victory over Napoleon at the Battle of Waterloo.

Originally hollow inside, it contained seating and a table within its circular walls until vandalism forced the council into the drastic action of permanently sealing it from the outside world. Although predominantly white, over the years White Nancy has seen a variety of colour schemes, including being painted drab green during World War II to prevent its use as a landmark for enemy bombers. More recently and unofficially, the colour schemes have involved a Union Jack and even a Christmas Pudding – but the jokers accomplishing these have never been caught!

Accessible from many points, the strenuous steep climb to this prominent landmark rewards the visitor with not only a sense of achievement but visual splendour as well. For a view of the sun's orb setting slowly over the great Cheshire Plain, this location would be hard to surpass.

VILLAGE LIFE

If you would be known, and not know, vegetate in a village;
if you would know, and not be known, live in a city.

———————————•———————————

Lacon, Charles Caleb Colton, 1780–1832

'Village life' – the phrase conjures up a mixture of differing thoughts among Cheshire people. It could be country inns bordering pretty village greens, beautiful sandstone churches with towers standing head and shoulders above quaint country cottages, or the audible 'thwack' of wood on willow as the local cricket team battles for honour in Sunday afternoon's match.

Cheshire is a county surely blessed with some of the finest villages in all England. From black and white Barthomley (*opposite*), to the picture-postcard scenes of Aldford (*inset*) and Great Budworth, their variety is astounding. Many are prized for their tranquillity and relative solitude, tucked away down quiet leafy little back lanes which only few visitors happen upon by chance. Others, too numerous to mention, are famed for their history or beauty, drawing day-trippers from far and wide to sample, if only temporarily, the delights of Cheshire village life.

Each area within the county displays its own building style and it is this that sets the scene for a huge variety of individualistic and often very attractive communities. Half-timbered walls and thatched roofs typify the south-west of the county, penned in by the border with Shropshire and Wales, whilst the central region sees red brick and slate dominating the landscape in villages such as Tiverton and Peckforton. The red bricks often appear inconsistent in colour due to the uneven firing they received during manufacture, and this variability, now known as 'Cheshire Brick', is widely sought after for modern-day construction.

Looking east we see the village landscape changing yet again, this time to that of the buff coloured sandstone often arduously quarried from open cast mines on the edge of Cheshire's Peak District and typified by the great silk and cotton mills constructed during the Industrial Revolution. Although the mills are now long gone, they have left behind the communities that grew up around their prosperity.

Regardless of where the villages are situated, they are noted for the warm hospitality of the folk that dwell there – and the high esteem held by the villagers themselves for their own slice of the county.

Bosley Locks and 'The Cloud'

Summer afternoon – summer afternoon ... the two most beautiful words in the English language.

Henry James, 1843–1916

Forming a barrier between the Cheshire Plain and the slopes of the Peak District National Park, the picturesque Macclesfield Canal meanders gently along for 27 miles through some of the most beautiful waterways scenery to be found anywhere in northern England. The 'Macc', as it's fondly known, forms part of the Cheshire Ring of canals, together with the Peak Forest, the Trent and Mersey and the Bridgewater canals. Built for the transportation of stone, coal, cotton and pottery, it was designed and surveyed by Thomas Telford and was completed in 1831, making it one of the last and, consequently, best-constructed canals to be built in Britain. Only one flight of narrow locks impedes the passage of boaters along its entire length. This lowers the canal by 120 ft through a system of twelve locks close to the village of Bosley, near Congleton.

Often described as the most attractive locks in the whole of England, the Bosley flight (*inset*) provides an idyllic setting for an enjoyable afternoon's walk. Summer sees large numbers of brightly painted narrowboats here and, together with the attractive regulation black and white lock gates, they provide a truly authentic image of a bygone era.

The local millstone grit or 'gritstone' was used extensively in the construction of the canal and its associated structures, including the lock chambers, bridges, wharves and even the former keeper's cottage alongside lock number one. Another delightful cottage is to be found beside lock five. The nameplate on its white-washed walls reads 'The Smithy', confirming that this indeed used to be the former blacksmith's cottage in the commercial days of the canal. Today, it is still maintained in excellent condition, and one can clearly see where the old stables used to be.

Towering over the locks at a height of 1,125 ft is the prominent landmark of Bosley Cloud (*opposite*). Marking the border between Cheshire and neighbouring Staffordshire, 'The Cloud' provides extensive panoramic views westwards towards the Welsh Hills and east over Cheshire's own slice of the Peak District National Park. Equally impressive is the view looking up at 'The Cloud' itself. Seasonal highlights include its slopes clad in the beautiful purple heather of summer or a pristine blanket of white snow in wintertime. No matter what the season, this majestic peak remains popular all year round with walkers, ornithologists and those enjoying the pastime of orienteering.

THE EDGE AT ALDERLEY

'Drink of this and take thy fill,
For the water falls by the Wizard's will.'

———————————●———————————

ANONYMOUS CARVING ON THE WIZARD'S WELL – date unknown

The Edge is a densely wooded sandstone escarpment rising 600 ft above the Cheshire Plain and boasting magnificent views of the Pennine Hills that form the eastern boundary of the county.

But the Edge is also so much more …

Steeped in legend and supernatural mystery, this ridgeline has long been associated with tales of wizards, warlocks and witches. Stories tell of the resting place for Merlin and the knights of King Arthur, sleeping silently beside their horses in an underground cavern hidden in the depths of the Edge, ready to awaken and save England from some future as yet undetermined catastrophe. Adding credence to this legend are the many caves, potholes and caverns scattered around the escarpment resulting from past copper and cobalt mining in the area.

The narrow trench-like entrance to one such cave system is known as 'The Devil's Grave', and it is said that anyone walking around the entrance seven times and repeating the Lord's Prayer backwards would summon the Devil himself to appear! The area has also provided inspiration for literary fiction in the form of Alan Garner's novel *The Wieredstone of Brisingamen*. Indeed, so much folklore is associated with the Edge, that interested readers will no doubt want to discover for themselves the secrets contained within its 200-acre area.

There are, however, many aspects of the Edge that can be viewed with one's own eyes, the Wizard's Well being one such location. To be found north-west of the Wizard public house, this feature consists of a natural spring whose waters tumble from a rocky

outcrop into a trough. A wizard's face is carved into the rock, along with an anonymous inscription.

Stormy Point (*opposite*) is another feature that is popular with visitors. A natural opening in the woods covering the northern face of the Edge, this bare sandstone bluff offers uninterrupted panoramic views over north-eastern Cheshire, Stockport and Greater Manchester.

GREAT HALLS OF CHESHIRE

The stately homes of England
How beautiful they stand!
Amidst their tall ancestral trees,
O'er all the pleasant land.

———————————————●———————————————

The Homes of England, FELICIA HEMANS, 1793–1835

Adlington, Arley, Capesthorne (*opposite*), Gawsworth (*inset*) and Tatton – these are just some of the famous names synonymous with great halls located in Cheshire. Owned in both the past and present by aristocrats and the landed gentry with famous family names such as Davenport, Bromley, Edgerton and Legh, these halls deserve a special mention. Here, though, we look not at the homes themselves, but at the landscape surrounding these famous buildings. Many will be familiar with the classic, often photographed views of their grand façades, featured in books, calendars, postcards and leaflets, but how many of us have stopped to wonder at the settings in which these elegant buildings stand?

Those dedicated souls trusted to look after these inspiring grounds have nurtured the landscape surrounding them with exhaustive amounts of loving care and attention. Over hundreds of years, men of vision such as the renowned Capability Brown have carefully selected and positioned specific trees to stand amongst the lakes, streams, follies and flowerbeds of these estates. Prime specimens of our English trees – oak, ash, elm and beech – stand shoulder to shoulder with exotic species such as the Japanese maple and Cedar of Lebanon, imported from the four corners of the globe.

Almost without exception the estates contain themed gardens with intriguing names such as the Japanese and Italian gardens at Tatton and 'The Grove' at Arley. Whatever the season and time of day, a

wealth of colours and texture have been exquisitely prepared to vie for the attention of visitors.

Perhaps the next time you visit such an estate you may forego the obligatory viewing of its impressive buildings, instead seeking out the hidden charms of its often overlooked surrounding landscape.

THE VILLAGE OF ASTBURY

And then my heart with pleasure fills,
And dances with the daffodils.

●

The Daffodils, WILLIAM WORDSWORTH, 1770–1850

One of the highlights of Cheshire's spring calendar must surely be the remarkable display of daffodils which adorn the triangular village green at Astbury, heralding the slackening grip of another winter.

Located just south of Congleton on the main A34, Astbury is fortunate in boasting a wonderful example of a traditional village green, now a rarity in modern-day Cheshire. On two sides are a number of picturesque brick and half-timbered former estate workers' houses and cottages dating mainly from the 18th century, with a particularly fine 17th-century black and white half-timbered cottage standing near the head of the village. Originally three dwellings, now only one, they have been lovingly converted into their present form whilst retaining much of the original character.

Commanding an elevated position at the apex of the green and complementing the traditional village appearance, stands one of the most famous of Cheshire churches. Dating from the 14th century, the Gothic-looking St Mary's is unusual in having not one, but two ancient towers. The west one, attached to the nave, was built around the 15th century. Pre-dating this, however, the north tower is of Norman origin and completely isolated from the nave of the church. It has a tall, recessed spire that was added some 300 years later, and it is this that gives the church its imposing appearance. Dramatically floodlit at night, it points like a finger of God towards the darkened heavens above.

Although springtime, with its remarkable floral exhibition, is the time of year for which the village has become justifiably famous, it is not the only season when it looks magnificent. After a heavy fall of snow, this exquisite place is once more turned into a landscape photographer's dream, creating the perfect winter's scene to rival any in the county.

CHELFORD

There is nothing ugly; I never saw an ugly thing in my life: for let the form of an object be what it may, – light, shade and perspective will always make it beautiful.

JOHN CONSTABLE, 1776–1837

Set amidst rolling countryside at the junction between the main Macclesfield to Knutsford and Alderley Edge to Holmes Chapel roads is the sprawling village of Chelford. It can justly be described as a village of two halves, as there is no single defined centre to the community but two distinct subdivisions with widely differing histories.

Founded at the site of a ford crossing Snape Brook, the parish

church of St John the Evangelist marks the original centre of the village. The current building dates from 1776 but its predecessor existed from before the dissolution of the monasteries in the 16th century. The crossing was originally known as Ceolla's Ford, a name that has been amended through the ages to give us today's Chelford.

To the north of Chelford, a water tower stands proudly in the fields (*opposite*) whilst Chelford's shop and post office is situated on the main A537 roundabout. Established in the 1850s, this is thought to be the oldest post office in Cheshire. One particularly appealing exterior feature is an old bicycle mounted adjacent to a top floor window that overflows with colourful blooms during the summer months (*inset*).

The Astle Estate, opposite the church, is renowned for its annual Astle Park Traction Engine Rally, which was started in 1965 by a few enthusiasts and these days attracts more than 30,000 visitors over its weekend.

The mid 19th century saw a major change in the structure of Chelford. The main Manchester to London railway line was routed north of the parish church to avoid encroaching upon the Astle Estate, and Chelford station was built. With excellent transport links a new community grew up around this area, which included two inns – the Dixon Arms and the Edgerton Arms – a village hall and, in 1911, the famous Chelford cattle market was founded. Now regarded as the centre of the true village, all five buildings remain, although the Dixon Arms, once a thriving coaching inn with stabling for 30 horses, lays abandoned, facing an uncertain future.

JODRELL BANK TELESCOPE

Look at the stars! look, look up at the skies!
O look at all the fire-folk sitting in the air!
The bright boroughs, the circle-citadels there!

The Starlight Night, GERARD MANLEY HOPKINS, 1844–89

One of the most famous landmarks in Cheshire must surely be that of the giant white Mark 1A radio telescope of Jodrell Bank belonging to the University of Manchester and situated close to the village of Goostrey. At 3,200 tons in weight and over 250 ft high, its vast dome-shaped dish has dominated the central skyline of the county since 1957, and when viewed from afar its graceful form is certainly one of the highlights of the Cheshire panorama. Often described as 'a marvel of engineering', it has been beaming back images of the heavens for over 45 years.

The science centre has, perhaps surprisingly, much to offer the landscape lover too. Open to the public, the grounds contain an excellent 35-acre arboretum boasting over 2,000 species of trees and shrubs, with many unusual kinds of heather a particular speciality. Arable farmland surrounding the science centre (*opposite*) provides a rich contrast to the tons of white steel girders that seemingly stretch towards the sky and, in spring, the pink and white blossom on the cherry trees delicately frames the might of this unusual structure.

Rivalling for the finest view of all, though, must surely be the silhouetted dome (*inset*) against a perfect Cheshire sunset, as observed from the main A535 road just south of Withington Green, between

Chelford and Holmes Chapel. Here the majestic form of Jodrell Bank's parabolic dish stands head and shoulders above the trees, dominating completely the rapidly approaching night sky.

ROSTHERNE MERE

I hear lake water lapping with low sounds by the shore …
I hear it in the deep heart's core.

●

The Lake Isle of Innisfree, W.B. YEATS, 1865–1939

Tucked away in a hidden valley close to the town of Knutsford is the enchanting nature reserve of Rostherne Mere. Surprisingly, this haven of tranquillity, the largest and deepest of Cheshire's meres, is to be discovered sandwiched between two of Cheshire's busiest arterial traffic routes. The A556 Northwich to Altrincham road to the west and the bustling M56 motorway to the north both carry hordes of people about their daily business, blissfully unaware of the magical stretch of water nearby.

For the wildlife of the area, a finer, safer place could not have been found in all of Cheshire. Under the control of English Nature, and with an absence of public footpaths, Rostherne Mere has effectively been sealed off from the general public – this allows the abundance of birdlife in transit or permanently inhabiting this oasis to positively thrive.

That is not to say, however, that the mere has nothing to offer the traveller seeking out the finer landscape views of Cheshire. Although it is possible to catch glimpses of this magnificent stretch of water when driving around the elevated leafy country lanes, there is a much finer way to view its splendour. Perched on the steep-sided southern edge of the mere, in a natural gap in the surrounding woods, is the splendid 18th-century parish church of Rostherne, St Mary's (*opposite*). It lies to the north of the village itself (*inset*), and was built to serve the religious needs of workers on nearby Tatton estate. The rear of the churchyard commands a superb vista of Rostherne Mere encased by trees that lead down to the tall, overgrown reed beds surrounding its shore.

The best time to view the mere is early on an autumnal morning when, after a clear night, the mist rises and dances above the warmer water, awaiting the first rays of sunlight to penetrate its very core and herald the start of another perfect Cheshire day.

LOWER PEOVER

What is a church? Our honest sexton tells,
Tis a tall building, with a tower and bells.

GEORGE CRABBE, 1754–1832

Cheshire abounds with countless charming small villages hidden away around quiet leafy little back lanes, and Lower Peover (pronounced Pee-ver) can certainly be included among them. Closer in size to a hamlet than a village, this rural community, which was founded on a stream called Peover Eye, hides itself away three miles south of the market town of Knutsford.

But discovering Lower Peover is effort well spent, for at the heart of this community is one of our county's true gems – the 14th-century St Oswald's (*inset*), described as one of England's most beautiful churches. Sitting at the end of an ancient cobbled lane called The Cobbles, the majesty of this black and white 'magpie' timber-framed structure and its picturesque setting create a remarkable impression. Treading the stone path beneath a black and white lychgate leads to heavy exterior entrance doors at the base of its 15th-century sandstone tower. Inside (*opposite*), one discovers huge octagonal wooden pillars, intricate medieval carvings and exposed timber frames supporting the pitched roof. Also on display is the oldest of St Oswald's artefacts, an ancient chest hewn out of a single solid trunk of oak.

Halfway along The Cobbles, we discover another of Lower Peover's historic buildings. Originally a medieval monastic preaching house, the Bells of Peover has been the village inn since 1569. One could be forgiven for thinking its name has something to do with the close proximity of St Oswald's church but this is not, in fact, the case. Formerly called the Warren de Tabley Arms, it became the Bells over a century ago in honour of the then landlord, George Bell, whose ghost is said to haunt the cellar.

Putting historic significance aside, the essence of Lower Peover remains that of a rural farming community and when travelling its pretty lanes one cannot fail to notice an abundance of arable farmland bordering the houses and cottages. Field patterns have changed little since the Middle Ages and, in summer, they overflow with the golden hues of wheat and barley.

GREAT BUDWORTH AND BUDWORTH MERE

I saw old Autumn in the misty morn
Stand shadowless like Silence, listening
To silence.

Ode: Autumn, THOMAS HOOD, 1799–1845

Situated three miles from the former salt town of Northwich, and set upon a low hill overlooking the scenic waters of Budworth Mere, is one of Cheshire's true treasures. Perhaps the most famous village in the county and once described as a rare bit of Tudor England, Great Budworth is a joy to discover, offering a vast array of charming, old-world dwellings presented along both sides of the main street.

Delightful half-timbered 'magpie' cottages nestle beside picturesque 17th-century red brick houses, with twisting chimneys, wide windows and eaves heading off in every conceivable direction. Summer is particularly appealing, when colourful climbing roses adorn the walls and the scent from the many carefully tended window boxes fills the air. Is it any wonder that this charming village, untouched by the ravages of time, plays host to so many television period costume dramas and films?

Great Budworth owes much of its character to the Edgerton-Warburton family of nearby Arley Hall and was almost entirely owned by them from the middle of the 15th century right up until the 1940s, when much of the Arley Estate was sold. In the 19th century Rowland Eyles Edgerton-Warburton, also known as the 'Rhyming Poet of Arley', was famed locally for his verses. Some of his poetry can still be seen around the village, inscribed upon signposts, inside the George and Dragon pub and above the old water pump housed at the foot of High Street.

Approaching the village centre, one encounters the magnificent sandstone church of St Mary and All Saints. This is the oldest surviving building in Great Budworth, with some parts dating from the 14th century. Silently watching over the small community, its tall, square tower is a landmark for miles around and dominates the village skyline when viewed from the placid waters of Budworth Mere.

Covering an area of 50 acres, the mere is set within the beautiful surroundings of Marbury Country Park, the former estate of the now sadly demolished Marbury Hall. Budworth Mere is a prime location for birdwatchers, who use the permanent hide overlooking its surface to catch glimpses of an impressive assortment of birdlife, including the great crested grebe. Although beautiful at any time of the day, the mere's finest spectacle is reserved for a cold pale Cheshire dawn when the rising mist dances above its calm waters, revealing Budworth Mere at its most enchanting.

THE RIVER WEAVER AND THE ANDERTON BOATLIFT

The bleak wind of March
Made her tremble and shiver;
But not the dark arch,
Or the black flowing river.

THOMAS HOOD, 1799-1845

Sourcing close to the village of Wrenbury, south-east of Nantwich, and meandering its way northwards for over 60 miles into the Mersey Basin, the Weaver is one of the county's most famous rivers, locked inexorably into Cheshire's history for its contribution towards the salt industry.

An Act of Parliament in 1721 sanctioned a section between Runcorn and Winsford to be widened and improved, subsequently becoming known as the Weaver Navigation. This enabled cheap Lancashire coal to be transported in great quantities to the county's famous salt pans, whilst also facilitating the movement of vast barges (up to 100 tons) containing the resulting salt products for export from the county. At its peak in the early 19th century, records show the transportation of over 200,000 tons of salt per year along this stretch of the river. An old soda ash factory (*opposite*), near Northwich, serves as a reminder of the River Weaver's industrial heritage.

Situated on a sweeping bend of the Weaver, close to the town of Northwich, the jewel in the crown of this great waterway must surely be the mighty Anderton boatlift (*inset*). A marvel of Victorian engineering, the lift provides a nostalgic reminder of the past importance of our canals in their heyday. Its purpose was to raise the working barges over a height of 50 ft from the Weaver Navigation to the Trent and Mersey Canal above, thus linking the boats to the rest of Britain's waterway network.

Having lain derelict for many years, this marvel of engineering underwent major refurbishment by the Waterways Agency in 2001, which returned it to prime working order. It is now used almost exclusively for the pleasure boating industry, and the lift is a major tourist attraction for the county.

WHITEGATE AND THE WHITEGATE WAY

Jog on, jog on the foot-path way,
And merrily hent the stile-a:
A merry heart goes all the day,
Your sad tires in a mile-a.

The Winter's Tale, WILLIAM SHAKESPEARE, 1564–1616

Marking the very centre of modern-day Cheshire is the delightful village of Whitegate. Here, set beside a charming village green, the quaint parish church of St Mary towers over a fine mix of majestic buildings and traditional cottages to create an enchanting scene.

Whitegate is best known, however, for being the site of the important 13th-century Cistercian abbey of Vale Royal, built by Edward I. There is a legend that, as a prince, Edward was caught up in a terrible storm at sea. As his ship was about to founder, he made a desperate promise that if he and the ship should survive he would build a monastery. The story goes that the ship made port and everyone disembarked, whereupon it promptly sank into the harbour. Edward was true to his word and, on accession to the throne, he immediately ordered the construction of Vale Royal Abbey, laying the foundation stone in 1277. It was dissolved, along with other monasteries in the 16th century. Much later during the 18th century, Sir Thomas Holcroft built a mansion on part of the site (*inset*). This building was passed through the Cholmondeley family right up to the 20th century, undergoing several transformations, including one by the famous local architect John Douglas (see also Aldford).

The Whitegate Way – a wildlife haven and relaxing cinder path walk through beautiful Cheshire countryside that once belonged to the Cistercian abbey – passes less than two miles from the village. This delightful route was formerly a railway branch line that was opened in June 1870 so that salt could be transported from mines at Winsford to the main Manchester line at the village of Cuddington, six miles to the north. The line operated successfully until 1966. Numerous public footpaths intersect and allow access to today's path, but a main entrance is via the former Whitegate station (*opposite*), where there are parking facilities (limited) and an information board. The old station and platform remain intact and are worthy of investigation – look out for the old load gauge.

Nature though, has to be the main attraction of this area, which has extensive hidden mine workings. Two water features, Sixes Hole and Marton Hole, both situated close to the Way, were created as a result of subsidence, providing ideal breeding grounds for birds that include swans and the little grebe. In conjunction with a careful conservation programme run mainly by volunteers, a wonderful environment for wildlife of all forms has evolved, drawing many visitors to this location.

APPLETON THORN

Up with fresh garlands this midsummer morn,
Up with red ribbons on Appleton Thorn.
Come lasses and lads to the Thorn Tree today
To bawm it and shout as ye bawm it 'Hurray'!

R.E. EDGERTON-WARBURTON, the 19th-century 'Rhyming Poet of Arley'

Should you happen upon Appleton Thorn during the morning of the third Saturday in June, then this could well be the song you hear echoing from the mouths of the young participants, to the tune of *Bonnie Dundee*. The 'Bawming Song' and its associated custom of 'bawming [or adorning] the Thorn' are unique in England. Whilst singing, village children decorate the famous Appleton Thorn Tree with flowers and ribbons before dancing around its base.

The original Appleton Thorn, from which the village takes its name, was planted here around 1178 by Adam de Dutton, a Norman knight returning from the crusades. On his way home he made a pilgrimage, a thanksgiving for his safe return, to Glastonbury Abbey, bringing back an offshoot of the famous Glastonbury Thorn said to have sprouted from Joseph of Arimathaea's staff. Although not the original Thorn, today's tree is also a cutting from the holy Glastonbury Thorn and was presented to the village in 1967. It was given National Heritage status in 2002, when the UK Tree Council designated it as one of fifty great British trees. The tree sits alongside the B5356 road at the main crossroads in the village, between the quaint parish church dedicated to St Cross dating from 1886 (*inset*) and the appropriately named Thorn Tree public house.

Appleton Thorn, however, can no longer be the quiet backwater of old. Both the M56 and M6 motorways pass within a mile or so of the village centre, and traffic in the form of lorries and vans, journeying to the large industrial estate established on the site of former wartime naval airfield HMS *Black Cap* now plagues its main road. Despite this, the village is still primarily that of a farming community, and the patchwork of fields surrounding it (*opposite*), supports both dairy and arable farming. Together with some attractively thatched cottages along the quiet lanes, the village maintains the air of rural Cheshire.

DARESBURY

*This time it vanished quiet slowly, beginning with the
end of the tail, and ending with the grin, which
remained some time after the rest of it had gone.*

———————————●———————————

Alice's Adventures in Wonderland, LEWIS CARROLL, 1832–98

Perhaps a bell-ringers' charter, the acrostic below, in which the first letters of the rhyme make up the name Daresbury, can be found hanging in the belfry of All Saints' parish church at the heart of the village. It is not, though, the reason why the 16th-century church draws countless visitors to this small Cheshire hamlet.

*'Dare not to come into this Sacred Place
All you good Ringers, but in awful Grace.
Ring not with Hatt, nor Spurs nor Insolence.
Each one that does, for every such offence
Shall forfeit Hatt or Spurs or Twelve Pence.
But who disturbs a Peal, the same offender
Unto the Box his Sixpence shall down Tender.
Rules such no doubt in every Church are used
You and your Bells that may not be abused.'*

ANON

In 1832 Daresbury's most celebrated citizen, Charles Lutwidge Dodgson, was born, son of the local vicar, at the parsonage in Morphany Lane. Better known to most as Lewis Carroll – the author of *Alice in Wonderland* – his memory is immortalised in the great east window of the church. Dedicated in 1934, the memorial window features many of the characters from this most famous of novels: the March Hare, the Mad Hatter, the Queen and Knave of Hearts, not to mention the most loved of all to Cheshire folk – the grinning Cheshire Cat – are all depicted in glorious stained glass.

The full story of the author's life can be studied a few hundred yards away from the church in the Ring O' Bells public house, a former coaching inn which now forms part of a Lewis Carroll exhibition centre.

As for the rest of the village, it remains the peaceful backwater farming community it has always been, thanks largely to the main A56 bypass road sweeping the traffic away to the west of the village.

Beyond the A56, the terrain falls away dramatically towards the Runcorn Basin and the River Mersey, and, nestling at the base of this hill, is the tranquil Bridgewater Canal with its neat little stone bridges and picturesque scenery.

Tucked away alongside the canal, can be found Daresbury's other well-known building, the somewhat unusually shaped Daresbury Nuclear Physics Research Laboratory (*opposite*). A distinctive example of modern architecture, it was opened in June 1967 by the then Prime Minister, Harold Wilson. The laboratory has played host to many of the country's leading scientists and research physicists.

ACTON BRIDGE

Summer pleasures they are gone like to visions every one
And the cloudy days of autumn and of winter cometh on
I tried to call them back but unbidden they are gone
Far away from heart and eye and forever far away.

JOHN CLARE, 1793–1864

The sleepy little community of Acton Bridge is probably best described as an idyllic commuter village, once famous for a plethora of pear orchards and dairy farms. Located in central Cheshire, four miles west of Northwich, it lies adjacent to the busy A49 trunk road that crosses the River Weaver before linking up with the county's motorway network to the north. The name is derived from Anglo-Saxon *ac* meaning 'oak' and *tun* meaning 'settlement', which when combined give us 'oak settlement' or a homestead in the oak forest – this being Delamere Forest.

As the second part of the village's name implies, it is perhaps the black and white bridge (*opposite*) spanning the River Weaver at the north-eastern boundary of the village that most Cheshire folk would associate with Acton Bridge. Replacing the original bridge, which had stood for hundreds of years a little upstream, it was built by Joseph Parks & Sons Ltd of Northwich and was officially opened to traffic in November 1933. With a span of 250 ft and weighing 800 tons, it was the first bridge in the country to rest on a floating pontoon, and was widely acclaimed as a marvel of engineering at that time.

For those willing to explore the area around Acton Bridge, there is much more on offer than first meets the eye. A network of paths and bridleways allows walkers easy access to the leafy lanes throughout the village, where delightful names such as Strawberry Lane, Pear Tree Lane and Orchard Avenue will be encountered, highlighting the past connection with fruit farming. In particular, Acton used to produce over twenty varieties of pear, including the 'Hessel' or 'Hazel' pear, and one of the village pubs takes its name from this.

Wandering slightly further afield, one discovers the picturesque Duddon Valley forming a natural northern border for the village. The

haunt of ramblers and ornithologists, this follows the course of the River Weaver with well-trodden pathways and passes beneath the magnificent Victorian 20-arch stone viaduct carrying the main Crewe to Warrington railway line. A delightful walk, which begins at the pontoon bridge, follows the eastern bank of the River Weaver northwards, sweeping walkers over the Duddon locks before entering the heart of the valley.

'MAGPIE' CHESHIRE

Nature is not a temple, but a workshop, and man's the workman in it.

IVAN TURGENEV, 1818–83

So many features combine to make Cheshire one of the most attractive counties in England. Undoubtedly though, the one characteristic that has come to symbolise it is the abundance of half-timbered black and white, so-called 'magpie', buildings within its borders.

Pretty cottages and churches cluster around village greens in a

display of traditional splendour, ancient farmhouses are scattered throughout the landscape, and some of the finest halls to be found anywhere in England nestle within their own parkland settings. A delight to discover, their black and white façades form the centrepiece for many a Cheshire picture-postcard scene.

Above all other 'magpie' buildings, the 15th-century Little Moreton Hall (*inset*), a moated Elizabethan manor house, is surely the finest example in all England, let alone the county of Cheshire. This often-photographed building with its intricate, reeling exterior is perhaps the best-known spectacle for Cheshire visitors, and it has seen little change since the mid 16th century. Now lovingly in the care of the National Trust, the house will remain unspoilt for all to enjoy.

Another example of magnificent medieval architecture is the distinctive church of St James and St Paul at Marton (*opposite*), near Capesthorne Hall. Dating from the mid 14th century, this splendid structure is reputed to be the oldest timber-framed church in Europe. Inside, a ladder leading to the bell tower is thought to be original and, during restoration work in the 19th century, medieval wall paintings were discovered whose outlines still remain on the west wall.

To single out one particular black and white cottage from the huge number on offer would be near impossible. Their delightful forms grace many a twist and turn in the county's roads. For the sheer wealth of examples displayed within a small area, though, the author must express his personal preference for the estate lands surrounding Peckforton Castle. A joy to behold, they represent an idyllic picture of Cheshire's enchanting 'magpie' past.

HELSBY AND FRODSHAM HILLS

There was a time when meadow, grove, and stream,
The earth, and every common sight,
To me did seem
Apparelled in celestial light,
The glory and the freshness of a dream.

———————————————•———————————————

Intimations of Immortality, WILLIAM WORDSWORTH, 1770–1850

Journeying in either direction along the M56 motorway linking Chester with the city of Manchester, one cannot fail to notice the two awesome escarpments of Helsby and Frodsham Hills. Over 400 ft high, these forested outcrops stand like sentinels towering above the flat expanse of the Mersey Basin and marking the northernmost reach of Cheshire's central sandstone ridgeline.

Whether Frodsham Hill is the correct name for the easternmost of the two is questionable, as it is also known by the names of Overton Hill and Beacon Hill. Not in doubt, however, is that man has seen fit to fortify these two commanding summits from as far back in time as the Iron Age. Remains of at least three hillforts from this period lie scattered around the two hillsides, and with a little basic mapwork they can be viewed from the many footpaths criss-crossing the area. One footpath is the popular Sandstone Trail that begins life here in Frodsham and ends some 32 miles south, near the town of Whitchurch.

Extensive views are available from many vantage points around the two ridgelines, but the finest is reserved for the position known as

Mersey View (*opposite*), marked by a needle-shaped war monument on top of Frodsham (or Beacon or Overton) Hill. During the Middle Ages, the vista from here would have incorporated the great royal hunting forest of Delamere, merging into marshland as it approached the Mersey estuary.

Today, the panorama on offer is radically different – though equally as impressive. Over the years, the forest has been scythed away to make room for modern day trappings. Frodsham town gives way to Frodsham Marshes, an area of great importance to ornithologists, with over 200 recorded species. Crossing the marsh are three important transport links in the form of the West Coast railway line, the M56 motorway and the Manchester Ship Canal. The oil refineries and power stations of Runcorn, Widnes and Stanlow take on a majestic appearance when viewed from afar, particularly at night when thousands of white lights shimmer and dance around the steel structures. Distant views include the entire Mersey Basin and Liverpool's famous city skyline and, on the clearest of days, even Blackpool Tower is discernible.

DELAMERE FOREST AND HATCHMERE

Of all the trees that grow so fair,
Old England to adorn,
Greater are none beneath the Sun,
Than Oak, and Ash, and Thorn.

---●---

Puck of Pook's Hill, RUDYARD KIPLING, 1865–1936

Long ago much of Cheshire was covered with forests. Over the subsequent thousands of years deforestation has taken place due to reclamation for farming and to supply shipbuilding and, mainly during the 15th and 16th centuries, the housing industry, evident in the many remaining examples of fine half-timbered houses scattered throughout the county.

But even as recently as medieval times, the Norman earls of Chester had a royal hunting forest stretching from Nantwich north to the Mersey estuary. Initially called the forest of Mondrum and Mara, the 13th-century earls gave it the name, Forest de la Mare – literally 'the forest of the lake'. Today, a shadow of its former size, grossing a mere 1,300 acres of oak, beech and coniferous trees, it is known to visitors as Delamere Forest.

Rigorous forest laws were the order of the day during the Norman era, when even the most minor offence carried extreme penalties. For instance, the sentence for being caught with a dog (even on a lead) in the royal forest was death. I'm sure today's annual half-million day-trippers to Delamere Forest would be aghast to be confronted by such bylaws!

In 1987 the forest was declared a Forest Park, and the Countryside Rangers of the Forestry Commission now look after both it and the increasing number of visitors. Their mission is to provide freedom of access throughout the area, with a hefty emphasis on conservation. Waymarked walks and trails whisk you off quickly to the depths of the county's largest forest, where wildlife abounds and activities such as walking, cycling, picnicking and horse riding are actively encouraged.

Lying on the eastern fringe of the forest, alongside the B5152 road, and edged with reeds, is the small stretch of water known as Hatchmere (*opposite*). This private nature reserve, owned and managed by the Cheshire Wildlife Trust, has been designated a

national Site of Special Scientific Interest due to the diverse make-up of bog, fen and woodland. The varied vegetation that such a habitat encourages attracts a multitude of wildlife. Perch, roach, bream and pike inhabit the water, testing the skill of the anglers that dot the sides of the mere throughout the year. Waterfowl such as the great crested grebe, mallard, mute swan and coot dwell amongst the reed beds, and seventeen species of damselfly and dragonfly have been recorded here.

EATON BY TARPOLEY

A thing of beauty is a joy forever:
Its loveliness increases; it will never
Pass into nothingness …

———————————•———————————

Endymion, JOHN KEATS, 1795–1821

Of the countless villages scattered throughout Cheshire, there are precious few that can be described as truly inspirational for both artists and photographers. Burton on the Wirral, Great Budworth and the former Eaton Estate village of Aldford are perhaps three – but Eaton by Tarpoley can certainly be counted amongst them.

This small hamlet, with its wealth of history, sits just a few miles north-east of Tarpoley itself and, together with neighbouring Rushton, has over twenty listed buildings within its bounds. Four particularly good black and white timber-framed houses remain, namely Hunters Close Cottage (*opposite*), Oak Tree Farmhouse, Well House Farmhouse and Church Cottage. All can be seen at close quarters, as each lies directly beside one of the many lanes that seem to emanate from the centre of the village like spokes on a wheel.

Standing at the crux of these leafy lanes and indeed in the very heart of the village, on the site of the former green, is the 'ancient preaching cross' (*inset*). This, though, is not all that it seems. The square, stepped base below the cross is certainly very old, and indeed is thought to have supported a truly ancient preaching cross – but today's cross could be described as a pretender to its stepped throne. Known locally as the 'Jubilee Cross', it was made from Peckforton stone in 1977 to commemorate the Queen's Silver Jubilee before finally being erected on the old pedestal in 1980. Often festooned with flowers, it makes a perfect centrepiece for the village.

Standing proudly in front of the cross is one of Eaton's fine thatched houses. Silver Birches Cottage was once the liveliest and most frequented building in the village; known then as the Alvanley Arms Inn, its cellar was hacked out of solid stone. The inn adopted the heraldic symbols of the local nobility to adorn its sign – the Alvanley crest supported by two blue hounds. This led to the inn's nickname, the Blue Dogs. De-licensed in 1885, it was converted into the delightful residence we see today.

One wonders what secrets the ancient base of the cross has been party to over the centuries, standing then as it did on the green in front of the village pub – if only it could talk!

BUNBURY

The sunlight on the garden
Hardens and grows cold,
We cannot cage the minute
Within its net of gold ...

Sunlight on the Garden, LOUIS MACNEICE, 1907–63

'Historic half-timbered thatched cottages set amidst rolling Cheshire countryside' might perhaps best describe Bunbury's delightful ambience. Here, reached by twisting tree-lined lanes, we discover a charming rural community possessing all the features expected of a quintessential English village.

The true heart of Bunbury must surely lie in the area surrounding its magnificent 14th-century sandstone church dedicated to St Boniface. Built on the apex of a hill and on the site of an 8th-century Saxon place of worship, it towers above old-world 'magpie'

cottages and distinctive red almshouses (*inset*) that nestle on the opposite side of the small leafy lane snaking its way around the perimeter of the churchyard. Inside there are many interesting features, including an ornate full-size alabaster effigy of Sir Hugh de Calveley completely suited in armour. Sir Hugh was responsible for rebuilding the church in 1385 and establishing a college within it. Look out for two small pirate gravestones lying close to the main entrance, one of which sports a skull and crossbones, and also a delightful stone carving of St Boniface himself set above a side entrance to the church.

Tradition plays a prominent role in village life here, and one discovers an abundance of black and white buildings enhancing the lanes. Church Bank Cottage, Little Orchard Cottage and The Chantry House are three particularly fine examples, and a special favourite of mine is enchanting Bunbury Cottage (*opposite*) with its splendid display of golden daffodils in spring. Tradition, though, extends beyond mere buildings, for Bunbury is also well known for its Wakes festival, which originated from the festival of St Boniface and dates back many centuries. An old handbill of 1808 states: '*Wanted, a person to conduct performances at Bunbury Wake ... It is necessary that he should have a complete knowledge of pony & donkey racing: wheelbarrow, bag, cock and pigeon racing, archery, single-stick, quoits, cricket, football, cocking, wrestling, bull and badger baiting, dog fighting, goose riding etc ...*'

One has to wonder if they ever managed to recruit such a knowledgeable person!

MARBURY

No stir of air was there,
Not so much life as on a summer's day
Robs not one light seed from the feathered grass,
But where the dead leaf fell, there did it rest.

Hyperion: A Fragment, JOHN KEATS, 1795–1821

The sleepy little village of Marbury lies amid rolling countryside, beautiful meres and tranquil leafy lanes in the most attractive part of southern Cheshire. This gem of a community could have been constructed with the landscape photographer or painter in mind – 'magpie' buildings, a lovely village green and perhaps one of the finest church locations to be found anywhere in our fair county combine to bestow a lasting impression upon any visitor.

Let us begin our brief tour of the village with the 13th-century, red

sandstone parish church of St Michael and All Angels. Standing atop a small knoll that seemingly rises from the waters of the so-called 'Big Mere', its graceful stature is best viewed from the public footpath skirting the eastern bank of the mere. On a day with little or no wind, early evening sunlight strikes its charming exterior casting a shimmering reflection into the calm waters. A closer inspection of the church reveals animals and flowers carved in two bands around the 63 ft high tower, which is giving cause for concern because of subsidence in the area. Gradually slipping downhill towards the waters of Big Mere, it is now more than two feet from the vertical.

Wandering back into the heart of Marbury, one encounters the village green. Surrounded by picturesque cottages, a smaller mere ('Little Mere', of course) and the pub, its most obvious feature is the large oak tree planted in 1815 to commemorate the Battle of Waterloo. Beneath its lofty branches, the Swan Inn has been quenching the thirst of the local farming community for hundreds of years, bringing about its own local rhyme:

'As long as the Swan sits by the Mere
There'll always be a pint of beer.'

Either side of the road leading north from the green one finds more black and white half-timbered buildings completing the idyllic appearance of this delightful village and offering an insight as to why Marbury so often wins the county's Best Kept Village award.

AUDLEM

*The Puritan hated bear-baiting, not because it gave pain to the bear,
but because it gave pleasure to the spectators.*

History of England, vol 1, THOMAS BABINGTON MACAULAY, 1800–59

Situated in the very south of the county, close to the Shropshire border is the historic little town of Audlem, although a much locally debated and age-old question is whether it is in fact a town at all. Receiving a charter for its own market in 1296 from Edward I enhanced its status as the area's market town, but in terms of size it would more aptly be described as a village – and ask the locals how they prefer to be known and the emphatic reply that greets you is 'villagers'!

Sited on a prominent mound at the heart of the town is the magnificent sandstone church of St James the Great (*inset*). The present building dates from the late 13th century, but the mound it occupies is possibly the site of an earlier Saxon place of worship. Standing on the main road at the entrance to the church steps is The Shambles, also known as the Market Hall or the Butter Market. All three names refer to an open structure dating from 1733, supported by eight stone 'Tuscan' columns under a slated roof. It was on this site that bear baiting took place during festivals and market days right up until the middle of the 19th century, when it was eventually outlawed. Lying beside The Shambles and serving as a permanent reminder to this practice is The Bear Stone, a large granite rock to which the bears were tethered. Other illustrious pursuits engaged in by local people in the past include bull baiting (also at The Shambles) and cock fighting at a pit in Soutars Lane.

Audlem has always been a farming community and some of the great farmhouses of the 16th and 17th centuries still survive today, among them Highfields, dated 1615 and located two miles south-east of Audlem, and Moss Hall (*opposite*) about a half-mile north-west of the town. Built in 1616, the latter is an impressive sight to behold with its perfect black and white half-timbered appearance. This can be viewed with ease after a short stroll northwards along the towpath of the Shropshire Union Canal.

The canal is a fitting place to conclude our tour of Audlem, for it is the 'Shroppie', as it is fondly known, that assisted its growth. It winds through the western edge of the town, and boats must pass through a system of 15 locks over $1\frac{1}{2}$ miles incorporating a 93 ft drop from Shropshire to the Cheshire Plain. Nine of these locks, between Audlem and Swanbach bridges, are known as The Thick, due to their unusually close proximity. Once the haunt of industrial barges, today the canal caters for large numbers of pleasure craft that use the 'Shroppie' for recreation.

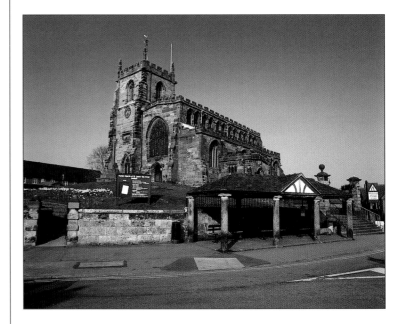

CHOLMONDELEY CASTLE

Oh, to be in England
Now that April's there,

Home Thoughts from Abroad, ROBERT BROWNING, 1812–89

Surely one of the most desirable sights to behold in the whole of southern Cheshire is the Gothic-looking Cholmondeley Castle (*opposite*). Situated four miles north-east of Malpas and close to the picturesque Bickerton Hills, this delightful estate belongs to one of the oldest families in the county. Deliberately built on the crest of a hill, the castle enjoys uninterrupted views out over its 800 acres of exquisite parkland landscaping.

The Cholmondeley family (pronounced 'Chum-lee') has been in residence here since the 12th century and the estate has passed through the male line for over 800 years. Most of the castle was designed by the 1st Marquess of Cholmondeley himself and was built from locally quarried sandstone between 1801 and 1804. It replaced an earlier hall built in 1571. The final touches, including the castellated battlements, were added on and off in the ensuing 20 years, culminating in the impressive structure we see today.

Below the castle are the gardens which many have described as being 'romantically beautiful'. Here the sweeping lawns, magnificent trees and colourful shrubs interspersed with attractive lakes provide the visitor with an awe-inspiring experience. The overall colour changes dramatically with the seasons, beginning with a mass of daffodils that herald the arrival of spring by carpeting the southern slopes of the castle. This annual display seemingly sets off a chain reaction within the rest of the grounds, with intriguing areas of the parkland bursting into life. From The Glade with its intricate 18th-century wrought-iron white gates, bright pink magnolia trees explode into bloom accompanied by a further display of white daffodils. Down in the Temple Water Garden (*inset*), complete with its bridges and waterfall, fruit trees delight with their red and white blossom brilliantly reflected in the still waters of a lake stocked with colourful koi carp.

No formal gardens would be complete without a fine selection of specimen trees and Cholmondeley Castle does not disappoint. Outstanding examples of mature trees from home and abroad abound. Cedar of Lebanon, sweet chestnut, lime, beech and some magnificent large spreading oaks all lend a hand to complete this perfect parkland setting.

MAIDEN CASTLE AND THE BICKERTON HILLS

A haunt of ancient Peace.

The Palace of Ar, ALFRED, LORD TENNYSON, 1809–92

It is hard to imagine a finer example of an Iron Age hillfort than that of Maiden Castle perched precariously on top of Bickerton Hill. The southernmost site in a chain of prehistoric earthworks covering Cheshire's sandstone ridgeline, this fortified settlement of 4000 BC boasted in its day both natural and artificial defences. To the north and west, commanding views over an almost sheer drop ensured the safety of all within its 1.3 acre enclosure, whilst to the south and east a ditch and double earth rampart, each over 10 ft in height and 20 ft wide, provided a strong deterrent for any marauders seeking to vanquish its residents.

Today, the earthworks can still clearly be seen, although diminished in size and coated with heather (*inset*). Marked by a stone plaque set at ground level, the site of Maiden Castle is open and free for all to explore, thanks largely to the efforts of the National Trust.

The Bickerton Hills, upon which the fort is set, are in effect a southerly extension of the Peckforton range, and this is a name generally given to the area of 283 acres of mixed woodland and heath incorporating Broxton Hill, Larkton Hill and Bickerton Hill itself. Significantly it remains one of the very few examples of surviving lowland heath in Cheshire, supporting a vast array of wildlife and vegetation, including birds rarely seen in the county, such as buzzards and kestrels.

To describe the area as a walker's paradise would not adequately convey its splendour. The combination of magnificent views and freedom of access via a multitude of paths and bridleways is the reason that people are drawn to this picturesque location in large numbers. Not surprisingly we find the famous Sandstone Trail here, once again traversing another of the county's most appealing locations. Hugging the steep northerly escarpment, it sweeps walkers across the three hills and through the heart of Maiden Castle before continuing south toward the Shropshire border some seven miles distant.

PECKFORTON CASTLE

No spring, nor summer beauty hath such grace,
As I have seen in one autumnal face.

Elegies: The Autumnal, JOHN DONNE, 1572–1631

The imposing Peckforton range of hills rises from the centre of the Cheshire Plain to a height of over 500 ft, and crowned upon the peak of one such hill, encased within its own small forest of tall trees, is the magnificent Peckforton Castle. The grandeur of its silhouetted form with its impressive round and hexagonal battlements stands like a beacon to be viewed from many miles around – but this castle is not all that it seems.

Medieval in style and with a disposition that any noble lord of that period would have been exhilarated to call his own, the casual observer would be forgiven for assigning a 12th or 13th-century date to Peckforton's construction. Remarkably, though, it actually dates from the Victorian era. Constructed between 1844 and 1851 by the MP John (later 1st Baron) Tollemache as his own residence, it was designed by Anthony Salvin, who previously restored the White Tower of the Tower of London and Windsor Castle.

Peckforton was built from the rock upon which it stands, quarried from less than a mile away and painstakingly transported up temporary tramways to its hilltop location. Sir Gilbert Scott, professor of architecture at the Royal Academy, said of the castle: '*... the largest and most carefully and learnedly executed Gothic mansion of the present day is not only a Castle in name but is a real and carefully constructed medieval fortress, capable of standing a siege from an Edwardian army ... the very height of masquerading.*'

Today, often used by film companies and documentary makers, the privately-owned castle is now a hotel and, with its extraordinarily romantic setting, is also one of the most popular venues for civil weddings in the whole of Cheshire.

GALLANTRY BANK

The first fall of snow is not only an event, but it is a magical event. You go to bed in one kind of world and wake up to find yourself in another quite different, if this is not enchantment, then where is it to be found?

Apes & Angels (1928), J. B. Priestley, 1894–1984

Mining is not an occupation people immediately associate with Cheshire, but nonetheless it has existed within the county for thousands of years since early man sought the raw materials for the region's numerous ancient hillforts. The Romans then mined salt from the centrally located 'wich towns', and later quarries such as those on Tegg's Nose near Macclesfield and The Cloud at Bosley were excavated to provide the gritstone and sandstone required for many of Cheshire's distinctive structures.

Perhaps a little less known are the copper mines that sprang up around the county. Those on the Edge near Alderley are well documented, but relatively unheard of are the copper mines of Gallantry Bank, near Bickerton, on the southern edge of the Peckforton Hills. The name Gallantry Bank itself has nothing to do with the mining activities of the area, but originates from 1640 when a local murderer named Holford was gibbeted here for his crimes, whereupon it became known as Gallows Tree Bank.

Mining began on the hill not long after this incident and continued on and off for over 200 years before the final demolition of its mine buildings and sealing of shafts in the late 1920s. The nature of the operation was erratic to say the least, owing to the marginal richness of copper veins below the surface and fluctuating price of ore. When high, the mines became a viable proposition and a profit was turned, but when it fell they would be closed for long periods.

Today, the area is a draw for ramblers eager to investigate the network of public footpaths criss-crossing its hillsides and all that remains of Gallantry Bank's industrial past is a solitary sandstone square-shaped copper mine chimney (*opposite*) dating from the height of operations around 1856. Standing firm against the ravages of time, its graceful stature can clearly be seen north of the main A534 road, two miles east of Broxton, serving to remind us of a time when man went to painstaking lengths in the pursuit of nature's valuable resources.

Beeston Castle

Castles in the air – they are easy to take refuge in. And easy to build, too.

The Master Builder, Henrik Ibsen, 1828–1906

Located north of the Peckforton Hills and standing directly opposite Peckforton Castle is Cheshire's most impressive fortification of all. Beeston Castle is the remains of a 13th-century fortress that silently dominates the skyline of central Cheshire. Seated upon its own craggy outcrop, a natural break in the mid Cheshire sandstone ridge, it rises almost 500 ft vertically from the green pastures of the plain below. Spectacular views abound from the inner bailey atop this ruined stronghold; indeed, it is possible to see a total of eight counties from here on a clear day.

Originally a Bronze Age hillfort some 4,000 years ago, this site has been garrisoned on and off right up until its final sacking by Parliamentarian troops in 1645 during the English Civil War. The castle as we see it today was built by the 6th Earl of Chester, Ranulf de Blunderville III, in 1225, imitating many he had heard about in the Holy Land crusades. Improvements by Edward I some 50 years later saw the complex strengthened and used in the line of defence for the war in the Welsh Borders.

One fascinating feature is the 370 ft deep well located within the walls, which was hewn out of the sandstone rock. Providing a fresh water supply, it helped the castle withstand sieges for much longer than would otherwise be the case. Folklore has it that Richard II hid a vast treasure of 20,000 marks in the well, but, despite several attempts to reveal its existence, it still eludes discovery.

Now in the care of English Heritage, the castle provides one of the most idyllic picnic locations to be found anywhere in the county.

DUDDON AND TARPORLEY

How sweet is harmless solitude!
What can its joys control?
Tumults and noise may not intrude,
To interrupt the soul.

Solitude, MARY MOLLINEUX, 1651–95

The lavender fields of Duddon village, three miles north-west of Tarporley, are the result of one thriving Cheshire cottage industry flying in the face of today's mass-produced markets. 'Cheshire Blue Lavender' was begun several years ago by the Evans family, who battle year in year out to preserve their successful niche market, and sell their produce to a growing number of valued customers during the height of our English summer.

Duddon's other claim to fame manifests itself (no pun intended) in the form of its reputedly haunted village inn. The Headless Woman derives its name from the ghost of Grace Trigg, a maid from nearby Hockenhall Hall who was beheaded by Cromwell's Parliamentary soldiers for refusing to hand over her mistress's jewellery. She picked up her head, tucked it under her arm and walked through a tunnel to Duddon Woods.

The village has links with nearby Tarporley, for it was the Baillie Hamilton family of Arderne Hall there who donated the land for the building of St Peter's church nearly 200 years ago.

Tarporley itself is an attractive commuter village with a trio of historic buildings defining its centre. The oldest is The Manor House, dated 1585, a delightful half-timbered residence that displays a colourful coat of arms upon one gable. Then there is the Swan Hotel on High Street, known to many as the headquarters for the famous Tarporley Hunt, with meetings being held in the renowned Hunt Room. Once an old coaching inn, its Georgian façade was built onto an earlier building in 1769.

The third building is the beautiful medieval church of St Helen. Its precise date is a little uncertain, as it underwent extensive restoration during the Victorian era. What is not in doubt, however, are the magnificent views of castles and hills offered from its southern side.

CHRISTLETON

Summers pleasures they are gone like to visions every one
And the cloudy days of autumn and of winter cometh on
I tried to call them back but unbidden they are gone
Far away from heart and eye and for ever far away.

Remembrances, JOHN CLARE, 1793–1864

Two popular interpretations of Christleton's name exist: one evolves from the early Anglo-Saxon village title of 'Cristetone', literally 'a cross by the *tun* or settlement, and a more recent one relates to 'Christ's little town'. Both of these correctly imply that it was the site of an early Christian community.

Today, though, very little of this rural village two miles south-east of Chester predates the mid-17th century, for it was here at the Old Hall in 1645 that the Parliamentarians set up headquarters for their attack on Royalist Chester during the English Civil War. Swift retribution came when the Royalists later sacked the village, leaving only the Old Hall, the Manor House and the 15th-century church of St James standing.

A visit to modern day Christleton, however, remains an enchanting experience, for this charming village has been rebuilt in true English style. The centrepiece is a triangular-shaped village green that is covered annually with a magnificent display of brightly coloured crocuses, heralding the start of another Cheshire spring. There are two features of note beside the green. The first is the village pump and pumphouse (*inset*) erected in 1886. The second is the towering parish church of St James, the fourth to occupy this site; this one dates from a sympathetic restoration during the 1870s.

On the northern outskirts of Christleton we find another focal point for the community in the form of the village pond (*opposite*). But ask a local where the pond is and they might throw you a quizzical stare as the residents' term for this small stretch of water is The Pit. An old marl pit during the 1400s, this mixture of clay and lime was dug out and utilised for the construction of Christleton's earliest dwellings. Nowadays, its setting couldn't be more congenial, with a multitude of waterfowl finding sanctuary amongst the reeds and the beauty of Dixon Cottages, former black and white almshouses dated 1865, reflected in its dark still waters.

ALDFORD

The frost performs its secret ministry,
Unhelped by any wind.

Frost at Midnight, SAMUEL TAYLOR COLERIDGE, 1772–1834

Situated on the eastern bank of the River Dee, approximately five miles south of Chester, Aldford is an appealing traditional estate village incorporating a long and varied history. It is part of the Eaton Estate, the seat of the Dukes of Westminster, and one is immediately struck by the uniformity of the quaint houses and cottages with low pitched roofs, twisting chimneystacks and heavily diamond patterned windows. Credit for the charming appearance of today's village has much to do with the 2nd Marquess of Westminster, Sir Richard Grosvenor, who was responsible for its restoration during the early 19th century, employing the services of Cheshire architect John Douglas.

The imposing sandstone church of St John the Baptist is also one of Douglas' buildings. Dominating the neatly laid out rows of houses that spread out below its square-shaped tower, it was built in 1866 but has the style and appearance of a 13th-century structure.

Aldford has two other features that any visitor to the village simply has to discover: Blobb Hill and the iron bridge (*opposite*), both of which can be seen from the public footpath found to the rear of the church, known as Marches Way. Blobb Hill is the area's best example of an old motte and bailey castle (*inset*), the remains of which date from the middle of the 12th century, and its main purpose would have been to defend the border against Welsh attacks that were prevalent at this time. Viewing the earthworks on a still winter's morning, with a combination of the sun's low angle and frost-laden bare trees, affords a truly eerie experience.

From here, a short walk north along the footpath brings you to the magnificent cast-iron bridge. Built in 1824 for Robert Grosvenor, 1st Marquess of Westminster, it spans the Dee on the site of an old ford used by the Roman road known as Watling Street. It was given the (translated) Saxon name of Old Ford, and it is from this that the village takes its name. With a single span of 151 ft, this exquisite bridge has the name of its engineer, William Hazeldine, written in raised lettering on the north side of its eastern end. When you stand on the bridge it is still possible to see large stones making up the old ford on the riverbed, but only when the water level is particularly low.

Burton in Wirral and Gibbet Mill

One to destroy, is murder by the law;
And gibbets keep the lifted hand in awe.

The Love of Fame, EDWARD YOUNG, 1683–1765

The enchanting village of Burton is situated on rising ground close to the Dee estuary at the south-west tip of the Wirral peninsula. It is a quintessentially English village, with a host of charming cottages either side of the road which meanders through. It is hard to believe that this quiet little place was once a thriving seaport, but this was the case for nearly 300 years during the Middle Ages, when the streets echoed to the sounds of passengers, sailors and troops using it as a stepping-stone to Ireland. By the 16th century, however, the silting up of the Dee sealed its fate as a port.

Today, many features combine to make this jewel in the Wirral a delight for visitors.

Standing tall above the village is the parish church of St Nicholas. It was built in 1721 using locally quarried red sandstone. Natural outcrops of this red stone also form the foundations for many of the village dwellings and are characteristic of Burton. Among the delightful cottages are those of Plessington and Sunnybank on The Rake (*opposite*), and also Barn End and Bishop Wilson's Cottage, which stand within 100 yards of one another along the main road. The former is a genuine cruck cottage with a black and white exterior, a perfectly thatched roof and window boxes overflowing with flowers during the summer months. Bishop Wilson's Cottage is thought to be at least 400 years old and was the birthplace in 1663 of Dr Thomas Wilson, the saintly Bishop of Sodor and Man. The cottage has an ancient ship's mast as the main supporting beam in the living room and one can still see the grooves cut by the chafing ropes.

Located three miles from Burton, along the A540, stands one of the last remaining windmills on the Wirral. Built in 1773, Gibbet Mill (*inset*) was a working mill for over 150 years and was later converted into a private house. Its present-day sails are a scaled-down version of the originals, but do not rotate. The unusual name originates from a gruesome murder that took place nearby in 1750, when three Irish labourers set upon a fourth, beating and robbing him and finally cutting his throat with a reaping hook. Unfortunately for them, they were seen and subsequently identified. One of the murderers turned King's evidence, and the other two were hung up in irons close to the scene of their crime.